Valmiki's Ramayan
Vol. 1

Retold by
Sunita Pant Bansal

Illustrated by
Suddhasattwa Basu

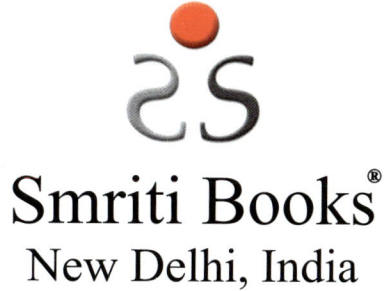

Smriti Books®
New Delhi, India

ISBN No: 81-87967-75-7

First Edition: 2006

© Smriti Books®

All rights reserved. No part of this publication may be reproduced or transmitted in any form or by any means, electronic or mechanical, including photocopying, recording or by any information storage and retrieval system, without permission in writing from the publishers.

Published by
Smriti Books®
An imprint of
SPB Enterprises Pvt. Ltd

Registered office
124, Siddharth Enclave
New Delhi-110014, India

Works
B-219, Sector-31
Noida 201303, U.P., India
Email: mail@smritibooks.com
Web: www.spbenterprises.net

Distributed by Shree Book Centre
8, Kakad Indl Estate, S. Keer Marg,
Matunga West, Mumbai- 400016.
Phone : 022-24377516
E-mail : shreebk@vsnl.com

Printed by
Excel Printers Pvt. Ltd.
C-205, Naraina Industrial Area - I
New Delhi, India
E-mail: pamekta@gmail.com

Contents

Introduction - 4

Ram: The Prince Of Ayodhya - 10

Kaikeyi's Two Wishes - 42

Bharat And The Wooden Sandals - 68

The Golden Deer - 100

The Brave Jatayu - 128

Introduction

Ramayan is a very long story of a prince named Ram. The entire story is condensed for little children in ten chapters, in two volumes. The five chapters in this volume are, *Ram: The Prince of Ayodhya; Kaikeyi's Two Wishes; Bharat And The Wooden Sandals; The Golden Deer* and *The Brave Jatayu*. Here in this introductory section, are the pictures of the main characters in the story. Instead of their names you will see these pictures. So as you read the story you will have to pause and identify the picture.

Dashrath  was the king of Ayodhya. He had three queens, Kaushalya, Kaikeyi and Sumitra.

Kaushalya  was the mother of **Ram**  **Kaikeyi**  was the mother of **Bharat**

Sumitra  was the mother of twins **Lakshman**  and **Shatrughan**  **Marich**  and **Subahu**  were demons. **Tataka**  was the mother of the demon Marich.

Janak  was the king of Mithila and the father of princess **Sita**

Manthara  was the hunch-backed maid of Queen Kaikeyi.

Sumantara was King Dashrath's chief minister and Ram's charioteer.

Ravan  was the ten-headed demon king of Lanka. **Surpanakha**  was the younger sister of Ravan.

Jatayu  was the king of vultures.

Kabandh  was turned into a demon by rishi Durvasa.

The story of Ram is the story of the fight between good and evil, with good winning in the end. Ram was a prince, but because of his father's promise to his stepmother, he had to spend fourteen years in the forest.

He had his wife and younger brother with him.

It was a time of adventure, when Ram and his brother helped a lot of people and killed a lot of demons.

In this book Ram's wife is kidnapped by Ravan, the king of demons. With his brother, Ram sets out to find her.

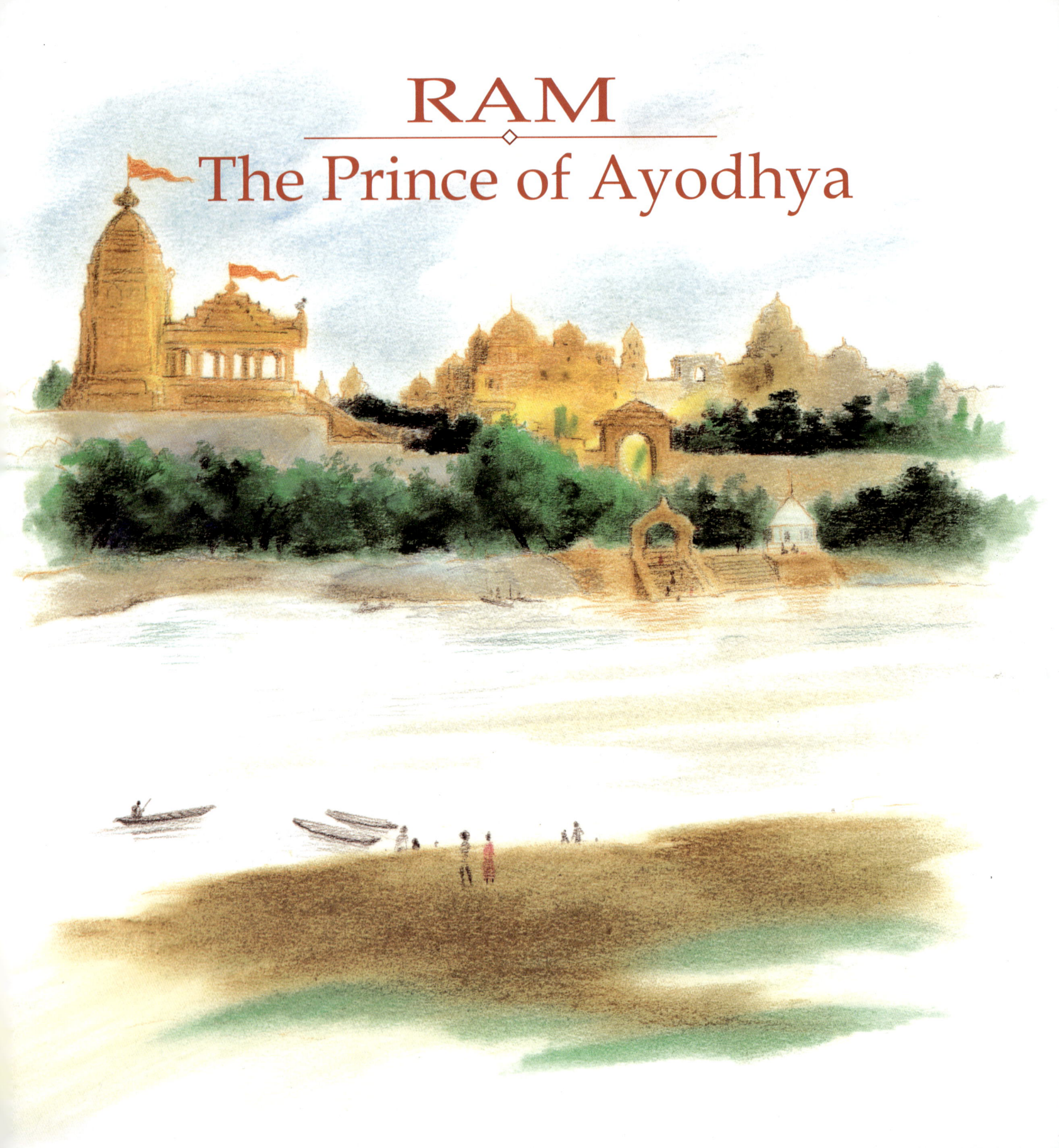

RAM
The Prince of Ayodhya

On the banks of river Sarayu, was the beautiful kingdom of Ayodhya.  the king of Ayodhya, was loved by his people. He had three queens   and  but no sons.

He was getting old and unhappy, and asked his royal priests for

help. They decided to do a big yagya to pray to Lord Brahma.

Now at this time all the gods were also talking to Lord Brahma.

 the great demon was troubling them. The gods requested that Lord Vishnu be sent to protect them. Lord Vishnu agreed to be born as  son of King  so that  could be killed.

After the yagya was over, the priests gave a bowl of kheer to King  The king gave half of it to Queen  and the remaining kheer to Queens  and

One year later, Queen  had a son ,  had a son ,

And  had twin sons,  And  The people of Ayodhya and all the gods were delighted.

King  was very happy indeed with his four princes. They grew up to be very bright young boys, but  was everyone's favourite.

always played together. And were always together.

Once the education of the princes was complete, King  started looking for suitable brides for his sons. Rishi Vishwamitra, the most powerful of all brahmins, lived in a forest near Ayodhya. One day he came to meet King  The king was very happy to receive him.

Treating him with great respect King  promised to do anything for the great rishi. The rishi said that his forest was full of demons, who did not allow him to worship. He wanted  to fight and kill them.

The king was worried as his son

was so young. But Vishwamitra told him that the demons belonged to  and could be killed only by  So King  kept his promise and sent and with the rishi to the forest.

On the way they were attacked by

 the mother of the demon   killed her with golden arrows. Then they reached Vishwamitra's ashram. For six days and nights the rishi prayed while  and  guarded him.

Suddenly two demons,  and  came.  shot at them with his arrows of fire.  was thrown a thousand miles away into the ocean and  was killed. Vishwamitra was very pleased. There were no demons in the forest any more.

As they began travelling again, on the way they saw a stone statue.  touched it. The statue turned into a woman. Her name was Ahilya. Many years ago rishi Gautam had turned her into stone.

Vishwamitra then took the two princes to the kingdom of

Mithila to meet King who had Lord Shiv's bow.

Shiv's bow was very heavy.

Nobody was able to lift it.

King  had announced that his daughter, the beautiful princess  would marry the man who could lift up Shiv's bow.  picked up the bow easily, bent it and broke it into two. King  was very happy.

On hearing the news, King  came to Mithila with princes  and   was married to  Her sister Urmila was married to   and  were married to the daughters of King 's brother.

King returned back happily

to Ayodhya with his sons and

their wives. Everyone in Ayodhya celebrated for many days.

Kaikeyi's Two Wishes

Once King  helped Lord Indra in fighting with the demons. He was badly hurt. The wheel of his chariot came off. Queen  fixed the wheel with her finger and saved the king. He was very happy and promised her two wishes.

Now King  was getting old.

He wanted his eldest son prince

 to become the king of Ayodhya. Everyone in the kingdom of Ayodhya was very happy to hear this news.

Everyone except  's hunch-backed maid.

When  was a small child, he was very naughty. He used to tease  about the camel like hump on her back. So  did not like him at all. She went to 's palace to inform her that King  had decided to make

 the king of Ayodhya.

Queen  was pleased to hear the news. But  insisted that 's mother Queen  would become the main queen. She would then treat  as her maid.

 would send 's son  away to another place. After  his son would become the king of Ayodhya.  would never be the king. So  should not become the king. 's son  should become the king of

Ayodhya.  liked the idea very much. She took off her jewels and started crying.

 cried so much that King  came running to her.

He asked her why she was so upset.

Queen  said that she would stop crying only if he would grant her the two wishes. The ones he had promised her when she saved his life. King  remembered his promise and said yes he would.

's first wish was, to make her son  the king of Ayodhya. Her second wish was, to send  to the Dandakaranya forest for fourteen years. King  could not believe his ears. He told  to change her mind and ask

for anything else. She said no,  should be sent away immediately. King  became very sad.

But  told his father not to

break his promise. All the people of Ayodhya were very unhappy, as  was their favourite prince. They wanted him to become their king.   told them that his brother,  would also be a very good king.

 said that it was important for him to help his father keep his

promise to   decided to go with his brother to the forest. 's wife  also insisted to go with her husband to the forest.

The three of them changed their clothes and took the blessings of King   Queens   and  They then left the palace with  the king's chief minister, in a golden chariot.

All the people of Ayodhya, even all the animals and birds tried to stop them. But   and  did not stop.

King   was very sad to see his favourite son go. He became very ill. Queen looked after him.

Bharat And The Wooden Sandals

When  was a young prince of the kingdom of Ayodhya, one day he went out to hunt on the banks of river Sarayu.

It was dark and  heard the sound of some animal drinking water from the river. He quickly shot an arrow at the sound, and heard the cry of a man.

The man was Shravan. He was filling water in a pot for his blind parents.  went running to him, but Shravan was dying. Before dying he told  where his parents lived.

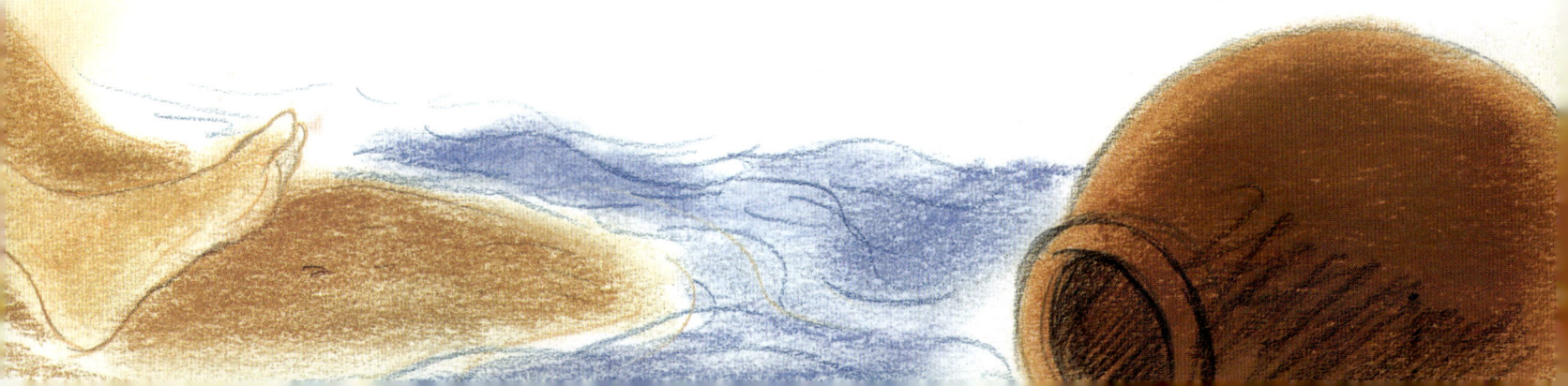

 took the pot of water to them. When he told them that he had killed their son by accident, they were very unhappy. They cursed him that he would die of broken heart for his son.

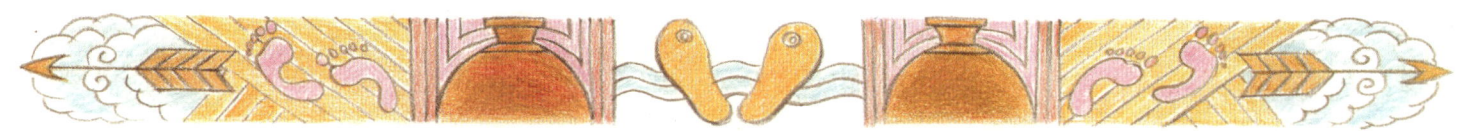

After telling this story to his wife, Queen  King  died. He could not live without his favourite son, prince

Meanwhile  his wife  and his brother  were on their way to Dandakaranya forest.

On reaching the banks of river Ganga,  told  who was driving their chariot, to go back.

After crossing the river in a boat,

  and  entered the forest. After walking for some time, they reached the ashram of rishi Bharadwaj. The rishi told them to go to Chitrakut, a beautiful mountain on the banks of river Yamuna.

So they went to Chitrakut, which was full of fruit trees.  made

a hut of green leaves and twigs

for the three of them to stay.

Now all this while the other two brothers of  princes  and  were visiting their uncle Yudhajit, brother of Queen  in the kingdom of Kekaya.

On King 's death, Queen  asked her son  to return back quickly. After getting  sent to the forest for fourteen years, she wanted  to be the king of Ayodhya.

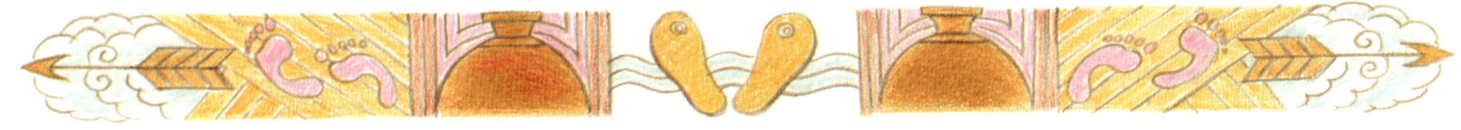

 and  returned to Ayodhya and saw that everyone was unhappy. Even the animals, birds and flowers were sad.  had made King  send  to Dandakaranya forest. After this, the king had died.

 was very upset with his mother. He did not agree to be the

king, as his stepbrother  son of Queen  was older than him.

decided to bring back.

The people of Ayodhya also went with him to request to return.

On reaching Chitrakut,  gave the sad news of their father, King 's death to  He requested  to return to Ayodhya as the king.  said that he would stay in the forest to fulfil their father's promise to his mother.

 told  to return back and look after Ayodhya, as their father had promised  to make her son the king. Hearing this  became very unhappy and asked  for his wooden sandals as a blessing.

 was a good brother. On coming back, he placed his elder brother 's sandals on the throne. He left the riches of the royal palace and lived in a hut. He ruled Ayodhya like this, waiting for  to return.

The Golden Deer

In Dandakaranya forest, while traveling,   and  came to a beautiful place called Panchavati. The rishis living there were being troubled by demons.

 and  decided to build a hut and live there to protect the rishis. The two brothers killed all the demons, making the rishis very happy. A number of years passed away like this.

One day  a demon woman, passed by Panchavati. She saw  and fell in love with him, and asked him to marry her.

said that he was already married to

 then asked  to marry her. He also refused, as he was also married. Getting very angry, she tried to attack  Seeing this  took out his sword and cut off 's nose and ears.

Screaming in pain,  ran to her brothers, the demons Khar and Dushan in the forest of Janasthan. They came with an army of fourteen thousand demons to kill  and

 took  to a cave to protect her.  fought the

demons with his powerful arrows

and killed them all in an hour.

So  went to her eldest brother,  the ten-headed demon king of Lanka. Hearing her story,  became very angry with  and decided to kidnap  to make her his wife.

 then went to meet the demon  who could take the form of any animal.  asked him to become a golden deer to tempt  But  was very scared.

Once when  had disturbed rishi Vishwamitra's yagya,  had shot at him throwing him a thousand miles away into the ocean. But  forced  into becoming a golden deer.

The golden deer went to 's hut. On seeing him  asked  to catch him for her. Leaving  to guard   went after the deer. The deer kept on running away from the hut, going deep into the forest.

Once they were very far away from the hut,  found out that the deer was a demon. He shot at him with a golden arrow, killing him quickly. But before dying the demon called out for  and  in 's voice.

Hearing the voice,  thought that her husband needed help. She got worried and told  to go and find .  agreed to go but made  promise that she would stay inside the hut.

Finding  alone in the hut,  went to her dressed as a rishi.  welcomed him and gave him fruits and water. Then  showed  his real self and asked her to marry him.

 told her that he would make her the queen of Lanka.

 refused and started crying.

As she cried for help,  quickly called for his golden chariot, picked her up and flew away towards his kingdom.

The Brave Jatayu

As  was flying in his chariot, , the king of vultures, heard 's cries and flew after them. He told  about 's strength. Once  would know who has taken away his wife  he would surely kill that person.

 told  to let go of  if he did not want to die. But  did not listen. Then  attacked  They started fighting. Finally  cut off 's wings and left him to die.

As they were leaving the forest,  saw some monkeys on top of a mountain. She dropped her jewels near them, hoping that it would help  to find her.

 took  to his kingdom of Lanka. He took her to his palace and asked her again to marry him.  refused. So he left her in Ashok grove, a beautiful garden in his palace.

It was a beautiful place but  was very unhappy. She did not know if  would be able to save her. She started praying. Lord Brahma heard her prayers and asked Lord Indra to go and meet

Lord Indra went to Lanka with Nidra, the goddess of sleep. While Nidra put to sleep all the demons

guarding the palace, Lord Indra

went in to meet

Lord Indra told  not to worry.  would certainly come to save her. Lord Vishnu had taken birth as  only to kill the demon king   was happy to hear this.

Now after killing the golden deer,  who was actually the demon  went back to his hut.

He met   on the way. They both found that ![] was not in the hut.

They ran here and there asking all the animals and trees about  No one could tell them anything.

Then they met  After telling them that  had kidnapped   died.

 and  went deeper into the forest. Suddenly their way was blocked by a giant demon. He lifted the two brothers easily in his two hands, planning to eat them.

But  and  were too fast for him. They quickly cut off his arms. The demon fell on the ground screaming in anger. He asked them who they were. They told him that they were  and  sons of King

The demon told them that his name was  and was actually a man. Once he disguised himself as a demon and troubled rishi Durvasa. The rishi cursed him to remain a demon forever.

 felt very sorry for his mischief, so the rishi told him that

only could help him. Since then he was waiting to meet

So now that  was there,

 requested him to bless him.

 blessed  who instantly became a normal man.

Then  told  and  to go to Rishyamuk Mountain near Lake Pampa. There lived the monkey-king Sugriv, who was the son of sun-god. He could help  to find

With the help of thousands of

monkeys, Sugriv could find

 and kill him. Saying this,

 finally died.

Something to think about...

Why was King Dashrath unhappy?

How did Lord Brahma help King Dashrath?

How many wives did King Dashrath have & how many sons?

Why did King Dashrath send prince Ram to the forest?

Who became the king of Ayodhya after King Dashrath died?

Why did Bharat want Ram's wooden sandals?

Who was Marich and why was he scared of Ram?

What did Lakshman do to Surpanakha and why?

Who was Ravan and why did he want to kidnap Sita?

Who was Jatayu and why did he fight with Ravan?

How did Lord Brahma help Sita?

Who was Kabandh and why did he help Ram?

Who all did Ram help in the forest and how?